SAVE OUR ANIMALS!

Blue Whale

Louise and Richard Spilsbury

Heinemann Library
Chicago, Illinois

Photo research by Hannah Taylor and Fiona Orbell
Designed by Michelle Lisseter and Ron Kamen
Printed in China, by South China Printing Co. Ltd.

10 09 08 07 06
10 9 8 7 6 5 4 3 2 1

Library of Congress Cataloging-in-Publication Data
Spilsbury, Louise.
Save the blue whale / Louise and Richard Spilsbury.
     p. cm. -- (Save our animals!)
Includes bibliographical references and index.
ISBN-10: 1-4034-7805-8 (library binding-hardcover) ISBN-10: 1-4034-7813-9 (pbk.)
   1. Blue whale--Juvenile literature. 2. Blue whale--Conservation
--Juvenile literature. I. Spilsbury, Richard, 1963- II. Title. III. Series.

QL737.C424S72 2006
599.5'248--dc22

2005027997

Acknowledgments
The author and publisher are grateful to the following for permission to reproduce copyright material: Ardea pp. **4** top (Y A Betrand), **5** top left (J Rajput), **11** (F Gohier), **26** (M Watson); Corbis p. **21** (P Johnson); Digital Vision p. **5** middle; Ecoscene pp. **12** (P Colla), **23** (S Donarchie); Empics/AP Photo pp. **15** (R Figuerdo), **27** (Maritime Safety Agency); FLPA/Minden Pictures p. **24** (F Nicklin); Getty Images p. **28** (S Chemin); Mariner Museum p. **16**; Naturepl.com pp.**4** bottom left, **7** (M Carwardine), **10** (D White), **13** (P R Gil), **14** (S Flood); NHPA p. **22** (B & C Alexander); Oxford Scientific pp. **4** middle, **5** top right, **6**, **9** (T De Roy), **19** (Survival), **29**; Save the Whales p. **25**; Still Pictures pp. **5** bottom, **17** (P Frischmuth), **18** (A & F Michler).

Cover photograph of blue whale, reproduced with permission of naturepl.com/Doc White.

The publishers would like to thank staff at Save the Whales for their assistance in the preparation of this book.

Every effort has been made to contact copyright holders of any material reproduced in this book. Any omissions will be rectified in subsequent printings if notice is given to the publisher.

Disclaimer
All Internet addresses (URLs) given in this book were valid at the time of going to press. However, due to the dynamic nature of the Internet, some addresses may have changed or ceased to exist since publication. While the author and the publishers regret any inconvenience this may cause readers, no responsibility for any such changes can be accepted by either the author or the publishers.

Some words are shown in bold, **like this.** You can find out what they mean by looking in the glossary.

Contents

Animals in Trouble

There are many different types, or **species**, of animals. Some species are in danger of becoming **extinct**. This means that all the animals from that species might die.

All the animals shown here are in danger of becoming extinct. These species need to be saved. The blue whale is one of them.

The Blue Whale

There are 83 **species** of whales in the world. Whales are giant **mammals** that live under water. They come up to the surface to breathe air.

Blue whales are the biggest animals that have ever lived on Earth.

An adult blue whale is as long as three buses.

tail

flipper

Blue whales have smooth gray-blue bodies. They swim by moving their wide tails. They turn by moving their flippers.

Where Can You Find Blue Whales?

Blue whales swim in deep oceans all over the world. In the winter, they swim to warm waters around the **Equator**. They have their babies in these warm waters.

This map shows where most blue whales are found in the winter and summer.

North Pole

NORTH AMERICA

USA

N
W E
S

ATLANTIC OCEAN

UK
EUROPE

ASIA

AFRICA

Equator

PACIFIC OCEAN

SOUTH AMERICA

INDIAN OCEAN

AUSTRALIA

winter

summer

0   2000 Miles
0   2000 Kilometers

SOUTHERN OCEAN

ANTARCTICA

South Pole

A blue whale has fat, called blubber, under its skin to keep it warm.

In the spring, blue whales move to the North and South **Poles**. There is a lot of food in the water for them to eat in the summer.

What Do Blue Whales Eat?

Blue whales only eat tiny animals called krill. Huge groups of krill float around in the ocean. A blue whale can eat 40 million krill each day.

A blue whale only eats during the summer.

Tiny krill get caught in the baleen in a whale's mouth.

A whale swallows a lot of water.
It uses its tongue to push the water
out of its mouth through its **baleen**.
The krill get trapped by the baleen.

Young Blue Whales

Female blue whales have their babies in the summer. A baby blue whale is called a **calf**. The calf is born under the water. The mother pushes it to the surface to breathe.

A newborn blue whale calf is as long as a small car.

Blue whale calves stay close to their mothers.

Blue whales are **mammals,** so the calf feeds on its mother's milk until it is eight months old. When it is a year old, the calf will start to eat krill.

Natural Dangers

More than half of all young blue whales die before they grow up. Some are not strong enough to swim in rough water. Some are killed by orcas (killer whales).

Groups of orcas will catch and eat a blue whale **calf** if they can.

No wild animals kill adult blue whales. They are too big and strong. Adult blue whales die when they get sick or old, or if they cannot find enough food.

This dead whale has been washed up on a beach.

Ships and Hunting

People used to hunt whales for their meat and fat, which is called blubber. Hunters chased the whales with ships and shot them with **harpoons**.

*In the past, whales were killed for their meat, blubber, and **baleen**.*

Big ships make a lot of noise under the water.

Blue whales pass on information underwater using whistling sounds. If **males** and **females** cannot hear and find each other, fewer babies will be born.

Dangers to the Blue Whale's World

There are many dangers for blue whales. Some people cause **pollution** in the oceans. Whales can choke if they swallow plastic bags, old fishing nets, or other garbage.

When people drop garbage in the ocean, it can harm ocean animals.

Smoke pollution in the sky stops warm air from floating away. The air makes oceans warmer and kills krill. There is less food for the blue whales.

Krill live in cold water. If they die, blue whales will die, too.

How Many Blue Whales Are There?

Blue whales swim in such deep water that they are hard to count. There might have been over 200,000 blue whales in the past. Today there are only about 10,000 left.

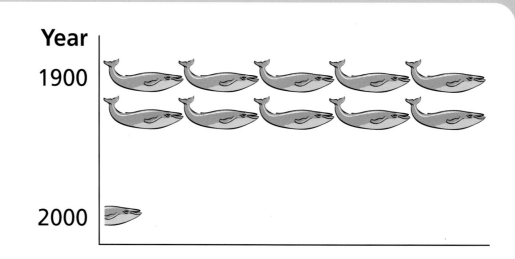

Year

1900

2000

This graph shows how many blue whales are left.

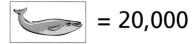 = 20,000

*Hunters still catch some **species** of whales, but they are not allowed to catch blue whales.*

Today it is against the law to hunt blue whales, but the number of blue whales has not grown. A **female** only has one **calf** every three years, and many calves die.

How Are Blue Whales Being Saved?

Governments in many countries are helping to stop people from hunting blue whales. They also stop fishing boats using nets and lines that could harm whales.

Fishing nets can be a danger to whales.

Governments are also trying to stop **pollution** in oceans. Some have set up **sanctuaries**. These are areas of ocean where whales can live safely.

These people are testing the water to check for pollution.

Who Is Helping Blue Whales?

Some groups of people raise money to save blue whales from becoming **extinct**. These groups pay people to study whales and find out how to help them.

This person is using a **harpoon** to put a tag on a blue whale to find out where it goes.

There are many **charities** that help blue whales. Save the Whales teaches children about blue whales, so the children can help save them in the future.

This man is teaching children about blue whales. He is showing them a whale's bone.

How Can You Help?

It is important to know that blue whales are in danger. Then you can learn how to help them. Read, watch, and find out all you can about blue whales.

There is so much we can all learn about blue whales.

Here are some things you can do
to help.

- Join a group, such as Save the
  Whales, that helps to save
  blue whales.
- Never leave any garbage on the
  beach or in the ocean. Plastic is
  especially dangerous to whales
  and other ocean animals.

The Future for Blue Whales

Some scientists think that blue whales may become **extinct** before 2050. It would be sad if these great creatures all died.

If blue whales die out, we would only see models of them in museums.

Other scientists believe there is hope for blue whales. There will be more **sanctuaries** for them. These places should keep blue whales safe.

When people pay to watch blue whales, their money is used for sanctuaries.

Blue Whale Facts

- Some blue whales live until they are 80 years old.
- A blue whale is longer than a Brontosaurus and a Tyrannosaurus Rex put end to end.
- A blue whale's heart is the size of a small car.
- A blue whale **calf** may drink up to 100 gallons (400 liters) of its mother's milk each day. That would fill 800 small cartons.

Find Out More

Murray, Julie. *Blue Whales*. Edina, MN: Buddy Books, 2005.

Spilsbury, Richard and Louise. *A Pod of Whales.* Chicago: Heinemann Library, 2004.

Web Sites

To find out more about Save the Whales, visit their Web site:

www.savethewhales.org

Glossary

baleen   part of the blue whale's mouth that works like a comb and catches food

calf   baby blue whale

charity   group that collects money to help animals or people in need

Equator   imaginary line that goes around the center of Earth

extinct   when all the animals in a species die out and the species no longer exists

female   animal that can become a mother when it grows up. Women and girls are female people.

government   people who run a country and have the power to make important changes

harpoon   sharp weapon, like a spear, that is shot from a harpoon gun

male   animal that can become a father when it grows up. Men and boys are male people.

mammal   animal that feeds its babies on the mother's milk and has some hair on its body

Poles   the North and South Poles are at opposite ends of Earth

pollution   when something makes the land, rivers, oceans, or air dirty

sanctuary   area of land or water that is protected to keep the animals living there safe

species   group of animals that can have young together

Index